Creatures of Legend

PHOENIX
ANCIENT EGYPT'S FIREBIRD

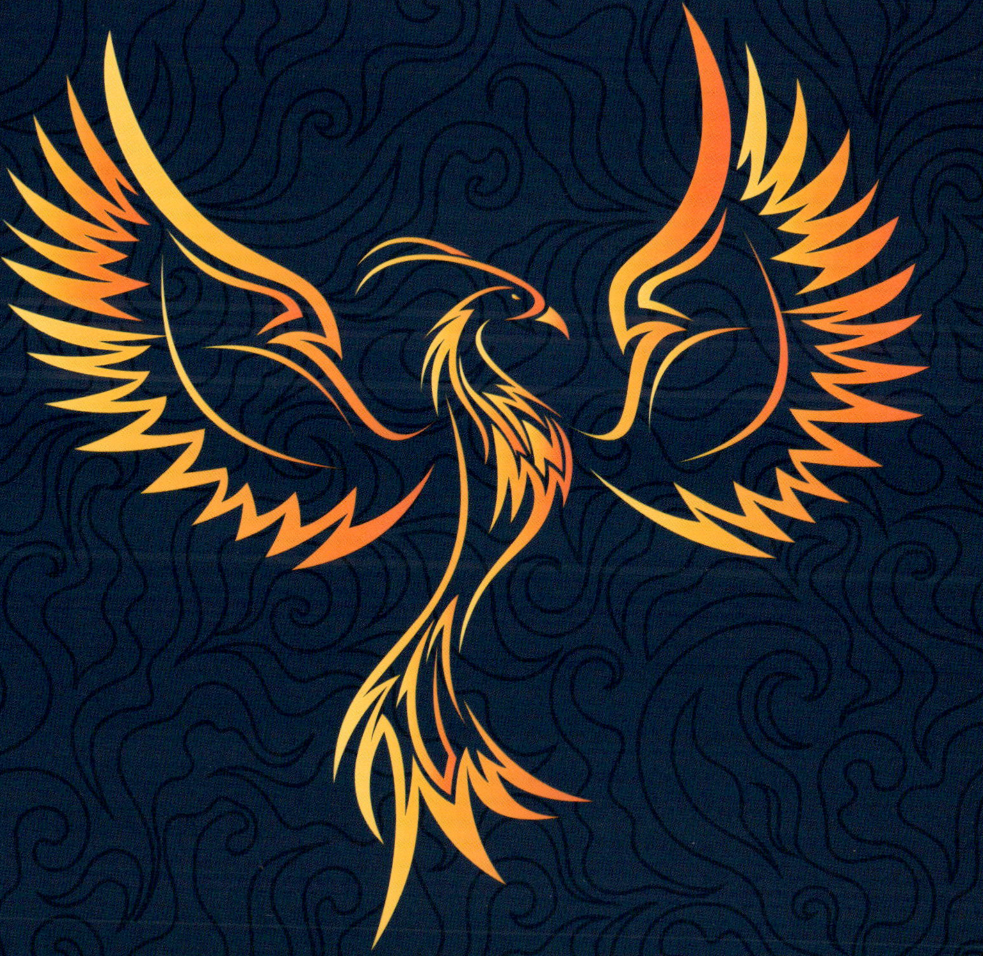

by Elizabeth Andrews

abdobooks.com

Published by Pop!, a division of ABDO, PO Box 398166, Minneapolis, Minnesota 55439. Copyright © 2023 by Abdo Consulting Group, Inc. International copyrights reserved in all countries. No part of this book may be reproduced in any form without written permission from the publisher. DiscoverRoo™ is a trademark and logo of Pop!.

Printed in the United States of America, North Mankato, Minnesota.

052022
092022

THIS BOOK CONTAINS RECYCLED MATERIALS

Cover Photo: Shutterstock Images
Interior Photos: Shutterstock Images, Getty Images, Gianni Dagli Orti/Shutterstock

Editor: Bridget O'Brien
Series Designer: Laura Graphenteen

Library of Congress Control Number: 2021951839
Publisher's Cataloging-in-Publication Data

Names: Andrews, Elizabeth, author.
Title: Phoenix: ancient Egypt's firebird / by Elizabeth Andrews
Other title: ancient Egypt's firebird
Description: Minneapolis, Minnesota : Pop, 2023 | Series: Creatures of legend | Includes online resources and index
Identifiers: ISBN 9781098242374 (lib. bdg.) | ISBN 9781098243074 (ebook)
Subjects: LCSH: Phoenix (Mythical bird)--Juvenile literature. | Animals, Mythical--Juvenile literature. | Animals--Folklore--Juvenile literature. | Fabled creatures--Juvenile literature.
Classification: DDC 001.944--dc23

WELCOME TO DiscoverRoo!

Pop open this book and you'll find QR codes loaded with information, so you can learn even more!

Scan this code* and others like it while you read, or visit the website below to make this book pop!

popbooksonline.com/phoenix

*Scanning QR codes requires a web-enabled smart device with a QR code reader app and a camera.

TABLE OF CONTENTS

CHAPTER 1
Fire in the Sky 4

CHAPTER 2
Power of the Phoenix. 8

CHAPTER 3
Flying Close to the Sun. 16

CHAPTER 4
Still Alive Today. 22

Making Connections. 30
Glossary 31
Index. 32
Online Resources 32

CHAPTER 1

FIRE IN THE SKY

Orange and yellow flames in the shape of a bird flying across the sky make people stop and stare. It is a magnificent sight that inspires anyone who sees it. The phoenix bird is on a mission. It is traveling all over the world collecting wood. It

WATCH A VIDEO HERE!

Some legends say the phoenix is made entirely of flames.

gathers cassia bark, frankincense, and myrrh in its rose-colored talons. Slowly the mythical bird's nest is built.

Red, orange, yellow, blue, and purple are all colors that show up naturally in fire.

The phoenix appears in many cultures around the world. It always **symbolizes** rebirth and renewal. The bird is known for building a nest as a **pyre** and lighting it on fire with its own flames. The bird and nest burn down to ash, and from that pile the phoenix rises again.

Humans have a natural desire to see something rise from ruin. People make mistakes. Sometimes things do not go according to plan. The phoenix is a physical representation of surviving those problems. It rises again. It sees another day. It still has time.

CHAPTER 2

POWER OF THE PHOENIX

The phoenix is a large, beautiful bird. Sometimes it looks like a **heron** and other times it may look like an eagle. Its eyes are said to be as blue as sapphires. The bird's feathers are usually red and gold, but might also be purple. No matter the colors, the feathers flame and glow.

LEARN MORE HERE!

Phoenixes have inspired art for thousands of years.

The phoenix can often look similar to a peacock in art.

> **DID YOU KNOW?**
> The phoenix may have been inspired by the golden pheasant, which is a brightly colored bird from China.

Every phoenix story says there is only ever one in existence. The bird lives for 500 years before it burns and begins again. Since the phoenix is reborn from its own ashes each time, it is **immortal**. There may only be one phoenix living at a time because the bird is so powerful.

The phoenix is famously known for having endless wisdom. It gained its knowledge because it has existed since the beginning of time. The first phoenix perched in the Tree of Knowledge in the Garden of Eden. Stories say all life began in the garden. It was also there that the phoenix first burned to ashes. It was allowed to rise again because it had followed the rules of the garden and never ate the tree's fruit.

The Garden of Eden was thought to be paradise on Earth.

Medieval bestiaries described creatures like phoenixes, winged horses, and three headed dogs.

The phoenix had great powers. Its tears could heal wounds and sicknesses.

And when it sang its birdsong, it was the most beautiful thing people had ever heard. The phoenix could control fire and had incredible strength and **endurance**. The bird was worthy of worship. Its reputation spread around the world.

MEDIEVAL BESTIARY

Medieval bestiaries were books made between 500 and 1500 CE. A bestiary was a collection of pictures and descriptions of real and mythical creatures, including the phoenix. Only the rich could afford bestiaries. The books were handwritten and painted. Sometimes they were decorated with real gold and silver.

CHAPTER 3
FLYING CLOSE TO THE SUN

The legend of the phoenix began in ancient Egypt. The bird was closely related to the sun god Ra. Egyptians worshiped Ra for all that he created. Every day, Ra would sail across the sky as the sun and die each time the sun set. He would rise again in the morning. The

DID YOU KNOW? Ancient Egyptians first called the firebird *Bennu*, which comes from another Egyptian word that means " to rise" or "to shine."

The disc atop Ra's head represents the sun.

phoenix had a similar story, but it would never leave the earth the same way Ra did.

EXPLORE LINKS HERE!

There was a city named Heliopolis in ancient Egypt. It was also called the City of the Sun and was dedicated to the worship of Ra. Heliopolis was a center for learning of all kinds. It had beautiful statues and a great **temple** for Ra. In the temple was a statue that the god Ra was thought to live within. The **priests** cared for the statue and had to keep it in perfect shape, otherwise the god would leave.

The phoenix was said to look like the sun rising when it took flight.

The city of Heliopolis was important to the phoenix as well. When the phoenix can tell it's nearing the end of its life cycle, it flies to Heliopolis. There it builds a

> **The phoenix was a symbol of wealth in ancient Egypt.**

DID YOU KNOW? There are rumors that 4,000-year-old remains of a seven-foot-tall **heron** were found in the land that once was ancient Egypt. This could have been the inspiration for the legend.

nest atop the temple of Ra. The phoenix uses all the good-smelling sticks and materials it gathered to create its nest.

After burning down and rising again, the phoenix packs the ashes into a **dense** egg. It places the egg at the feet of Ra's statue. From there, the great bird flies away singing its beautiful song proudly around the world.

CHAPTER 4

STILL ALIVE TODAY

Many cultures adopted the myth of the phoenix after it began as *Bennu* in ancient Egypt. The Greeks were the first to follow. Their phoenix was not related to their sun god,

COMPLETE AN ACTIVITY HERE!

Helios. But it was said that the bird's song was so beautiful that even Helios would stop his chariot to listen.

Helios is the sun god in ancient Greek culture.

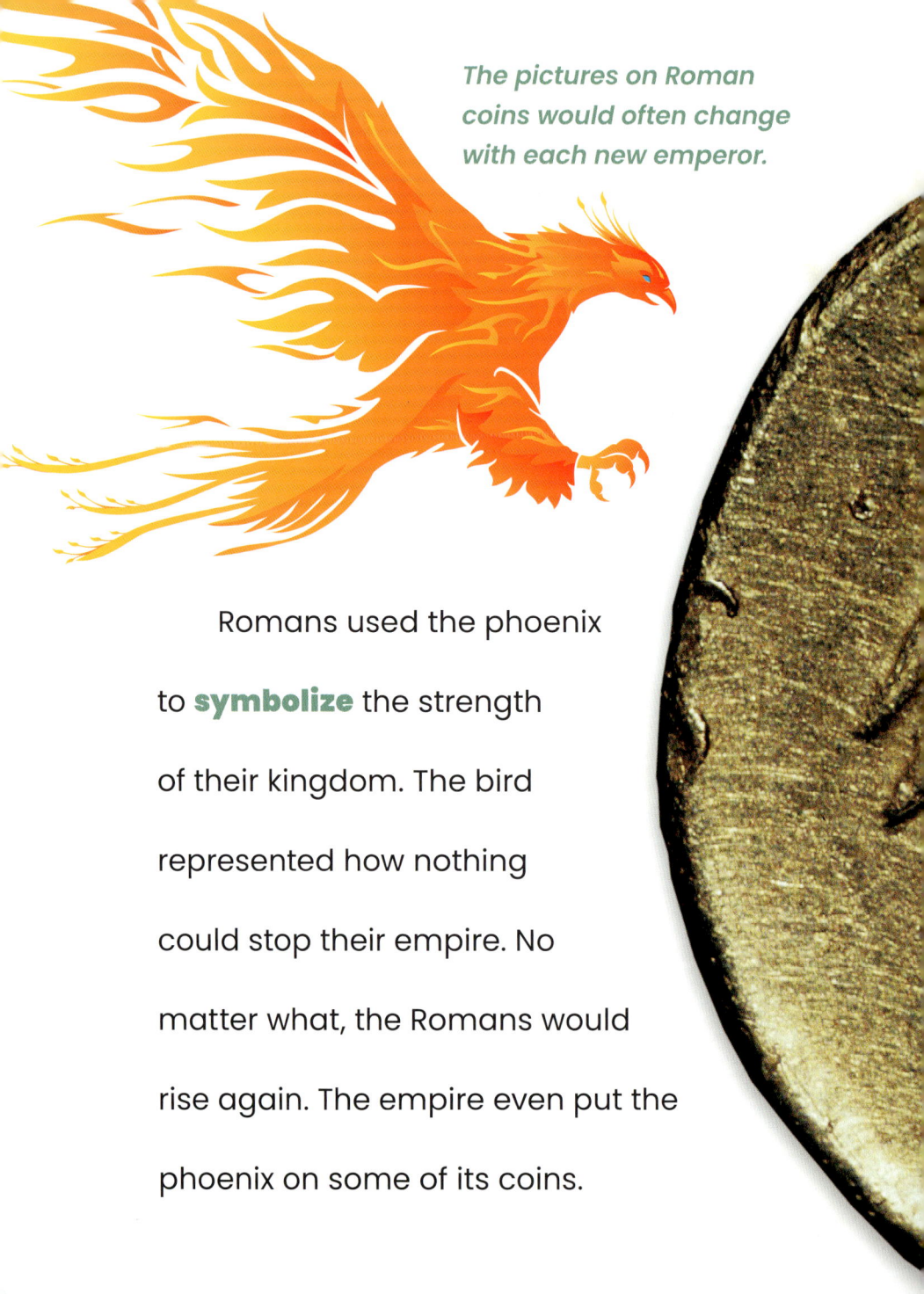

The pictures on Roman coins would often change with each new emperor.

Romans used the phoenix to **symbolize** the strength of their kingdom. The bird represented how nothing could stop their empire. No matter what, the Romans would rise again. The empire even put the phoenix on some of its coins.

In one Persian legend, the simurgh rescues a human child and raises the child as its own.

In the Persian Empire, there was a giant legendary bird called the *simurgh*. It shares many characteristics with the phoenix. The *simurgh* is **immortal** and holds all the knowledge in the world. Stories say this version of the phoenix lived through the destruction of the world three times.

The simurgh was thought to clean water and land.

Today, the phoenix is represented in many places. It is the name of a city in Arizona. The Harry Potter novels include a phoenix named Fawkes that has healing tears and burns to ashes. Some wands in Harry Potter contain phoenix feathers. There is also a Pokémon character modeled after the legendary bird.

Cassia Bark: A spice made from the bark of East Asian evergreens. It is spiritually healing and protective.

Nard: An herb from the Himalayas. It is used in medicines, perfumes, and ceremonies to lift spirits.

Myrrh: A strong-smelling **resin** from certain trees in the Middle East. It holds the nest together. Myrrh is thought to form a connection between heaven and earth.

WHAT MAKES UP THE PHOENIX NEST?

MAKING CONNECTIONS

TEXT-TO-SELF

How would you react if you saw a phoenix flying in the sky? Write a few sentences explaining your answer.

TEXT-TO-TEXT

Have you read any books about different legendary creatures? How were those creatures similar to and different from the phoenix?

TEXT-TO-WORLD

The phoenix symbolizes renewal and rebirth. Why do you think humans are interested in those two symbols?

GLOSSARY

dense — having parts very close together with little space between.

endurance — the ability to go on under pain or hardship.

heron — any of the long-necked and long-legged birds that spend time standing in shallow water.

immortal — someone or something that will not die.

priest — someone who performs official religious ceremonies.

pyre — a pile of material to be burned.

resin — a sticky substance produced by evergreen trees and certain other plants.

symbol — an object or picture that represents something else.

temple — a building or place where a god or gods are worshiped.

INDEX

appearance, 4, 8

ashes, 7, 11–12, 21, 28

bestiary, 15

Egypt, 16–22

fire, 4, 7–8, 15

Greeks, 22–23

Harry Potter, 28

nest, 5, 7, 21, 29

Romans, 24

symbol, 6, 24

Scan this code* and others like it while you read, or visit the website below to make this book pop!

popbooksonline.com/phoenix

*Scanning QR codes requires a web-enabled smart device with a QR code reader app and a camera.